Recess

Sherry L. Blanchard & Suzanne Lussier
Bradford, Maine

Illustrations by
Steve Pileggi

Dominie Press, Inc.

The development of the *Teacher's Choice Series* was supported by the Reading Recovery project at California State University, San Bernardino. All authors' royalties from the sale of the *Teacher's Choice Series* will be used to support various Reading Recovery projects.

Publisher: Raymond Yuen
Series Editor: Stanley L. Swartz
Illustrator: Steve Pileggi
Cover Designer: Steve Morris
Page Design: Pamela S. Pettigrew

Copyright © 1996 Dominie Press, Inc. All rights reserved. No part of this publication may be reproduced or transmitted in any form or by any means without permission in writing from the publisher. Reproduction of any part of this book, through photocopy, recording, or any electronic or mechanical retrieval system, without the written permission of the publisher is an infringement of the copyright law.

Published by:

℗ Dominie Press, Inc.

1949 Kellogg Avenue
Carlsbad, California 92008 USA

ISBN 1-56270-550-4

Printed in Singapore
9 10 11 12 13 VoZF 14 13 12 11 10

We play jacks.

We play marbles.

We play dodgeball.

We play hopscotch.

We play four-square.

We play kickball.

We play tag.

We play…together!

About the Authors

Sherry L. Blanchard earned her B.S. in Education at the University of Maine at Orono in 1987. She has taught for 9 years and is currently a Grade 1 teacher at Bradford Elementary School in Maine. Sherry lives in East Corinth, Maine where she enjoys reading and sports, in particular, snowmobiling.

Suzanne R. Lussier attended Plymouth State College in New Hampshire where she earned a B.S. in Education in 1972. In 1989, she received her Masters in Computer Education from Lesley College in Cambridge, Massachusettes. She has taught for 23 years and currently teaches Reading Recovery™ and Grade 5 Writing at Bradford Elementary School in Maine. Suzanne resides in Charleston, Maine and enjoys skiing, biking, hiking, nature studies, photography, and stained glass.